Inside Reading 2

THE ACADEMIC WORD LIST IN CONTEXT

Instructor's Pack

By Lawrence J. Zwier
Series Director: Cheryl Boyd Zimmerman

OXFORD
UNIVERSITY PRESS

OXFORD
UNIVERSITY PRESS

198 Madison Avenue
New York, NY 10016 USA

Great Clarendon Street, Oxford OX2 6DP UK

Oxford University Press is a department of the University of Oxford.
It furthers the University's objective of excellence in research, scholarship,
and education by publishing worldwide in

Oxford   New York
Auckland   Cape Town   Dar es Salaam   Hong Kong   Karachi
Kuala Lumpur   Madrid   Melbourne   Mexico City   Nairobi
New Delhi   Shanghai   Taipei   Toronto

With offices in
Argentina   Austria   Brazil   Chile   Czech Republic   France   Greece
Guatemala   Hungary   Italy   Japan   Poland   Portugal   Singapore
South Korea   Switzerland   Thailand   Turkey   Ukraine   Vietnam

OXFORD and OXFORD ENGLISH are registered trademarks of
Oxford University Press.

© Oxford University Press 2009

Database right Oxford University Press (maker)

Editorial Director: Sally Yagan
Senior Managing Editor: Patricia O'Neill
Editor: Dena Daniel
Associate Development Editor: Olga Christopoulos
Art Director: Robert Carangelo
Design Manager: Maj-Britt Hagsted
Production Artist: Julie Armstrong
Compositor: TSI Graphics Inc.
Cover design: Stacy Merlin
Manufacturing Manager: Shanta Persaud
Manufacturing Controller: Eve Wong

Instructor's Pack
ISBN: 978 0 19 441621 4
Answer Key Booklet
ISBN: 978 0 19 441604 7

Printed in Hong Kong

10   9   8   7   6   5   4   3   2   1

Contents

Answer Key

To the Teacher

There is a natural relationship between academic reading and word learning. *Inside Reading* is a four-level reading and vocabulary series designed to use this relationship to best advantage. Through principled instruction and practice with reading strategies and skills, students will increase their ability to comprehend reading material. Likewise, through a principled approach to the complex nature of vocabulary knowledge, learners will better understand how to make sense of the complex nature of academic word learning. *Inside Reading 2* is intended for students at the intermediate level.

Academic Reading and Vocabulary: A Reciprocal Relationship

In the beginning stages of language learning, when the learner is making simple connections between familiar oral words and written forms, vocabulary knowledge plays a crucial role. In later stages, such as those addressed by *Inside Reading*, word learning and reading are increasingly interdependent: rich word knowledge facilitates reading, and effective reading skills facilitate vocabulary comprehension and learning.[1]

The word knowledge that is needed by the reader in this reciprocal process is more than knowledge of definitions.[2] Truly knowing a word well enough to use it in reading (as well as in production) means knowing something about its grammar, word forms, collocations, register, associations, and a great deal about its meaning, including its connotations and multiple meanings.[3] Any of this information may be called upon to help the reader make the inferences needed to understand the word's meaning in a particular text. For example, a passage's meaning can be controlled completely by a connotation

  She was *frugal*. (positive connotation)
  She was *stingy*. (negative connotation)
by grammatical form
  He valued his *memory*.
  He valued his *memories*.

or an alternate meaning
  The *labor* was intense. (physical work vs. childbirth)

Inside Reading recognizes the complexity of knowing a word. Students are given frequent and varied practice with all aspects of word knowledge. Vocabulary activities are closely related in topic to the reading selections, providing multiple exposures to a word in actual use and opportunities to work with its meanings, grammatical features, word forms, collocations, register, and associations.

To join principled vocabulary instruction with academic reading instruction is both natural and effective. *Inside Reading* is designed to address the reciprocal relationship between reading and vocabulary and to use it to help students develop academic proficiency.

A Closer Look at Academic Reading

Students preparing for academic work benefit from instruction that includes attention to the language as well as attention to the process of reading. The Interactive Reading model indicates that reading is an active process in which readers draw upon *top-down processing* (bringing meaning to the text), as well as *bottom-up processing* (decoding words and other details of language).[4]

The *top-down* aspect of this construct suggests that reading is facilitated by interesting and relevant reading materials that activate a range of knowledge in a reader's mind, knowledge that is refined and extended during the act of reading.

The *bottom-up* aspect of this model suggests that the learner needs to pay attention to language proficiency, including vocabulary. An academic reading course must address the teaching of higher-level reading strategies without neglecting the need for language support.[5]

---

[1] Koda, 2005

[2] See the meta-analysis of L1 vocabulary studies by Stahl & Fairbanks, 1986.

[3] Nation, 1990

[4] Carrell, Devine, and Eskey, 1988

[5] Birch, 2002; Eskey, 1988

Inside Reading addresses both sides of the interactive model. High-interest academic readings and activities provide students with opportunities to draw upon life experience in their mastery of a wide variety of strategies and skills, including

- previewing
- scanning
- using context clues to clarify meaning
- finding the main idea
- summarizing
- making inferences.

Rich vocabulary instruction and practice that targets vocabulary from the Academic Word List (AWL) provide opportunities for students to improve their language proficiency and their ability to decode and process vocabulary.

A Closer Look at Academic Vocabulary

Academic vocabulary consists of those words which are used broadly in all academic domains, but are not necessarily frequent in other domains. They are words in the academic register that are needed by students who intend to pursue higher education. They are not the technical words used in one academic field or another (e.g., *genetics, fiduciary, proton*), but are found in all academic areas, often in a supportive role (*substitute, function, inhibit*).

The most principled and widely accepted list of academic words to date is The Academic Word List (AWL), compiled by Averil Coxhead in 2000. Its selection was based on a corpus of 3.5 million words of running text from academic materials across four academic disciplines: the humanities, business, law, and the physical and life sciences. The criteria for selection of the 570 word families on the AWL was that the words appear frequently and uniformly across a wide range of academic texts, and that they not appear among the first 2000 most common words of English, as identified by the General Service List.[6]

Across the four levels of *Inside Reading*, students are introduced to the 570 word families of the AWL

at a gradual pace of about 15 words per unit. Their usage is authentic, the readings in which they appear are high interest, and the words are practiced and recycled in a variety of activities, facilitating both reading comprehension and word learning.

There has been a great deal of research into the optimal classroom conditions for facilitating word learning. This research points to several key factors.

Noticing: Before new words can be learned, they must be noticed. Schmidt, in his well-known *noticing hypothesis*, states

> noticing is the necessary and sufficient condition for converting input into intake. Incidental learning, on the other hand, is clearly both possible and effective when the demands of a task focus attention on what is to be learned.[7]

Inside Reading facilitates noticing in two ways. Target words are printed in boldface type at their first occurrence to draw the students' attention to their context, usage, and word form. Students are then offered repeated opportunities to focus on them in activities and discussions. *Inside Reading* also devotes activities and tasks to particular target words. This is often accompanied by a presentation box giving information about the word, its family members, and its usage.

Teachers can further facilitate noticing by pre-teaching selected words through "rich instruction," meaning instruction that focuses on what it means to know a word, looks at the word in more than one setting, and involves learners in actively processing the word.[8] *Inside Reading* facilitates rich instruction by providing engaging activities that use and spotlight target words in both written and oral practice.

Repetition: Word learning is incremental. A learner is able to pick up new knowledge about a word with each encounter. Repetition also assists learner memory—multiple exposures at varying intervals dramatically enhance retention.

Repetition alone doesn't account for learning; the types and intervals of repetitions are also important.

---

[6] West, 1953; Coxhead 2000
[7] Schmidt, 1990, p. 129
[8] Nation, 2001, p. 157

Research shows that words are best retained when the practice with a new word is brief but the word is repeated several times at increasing intervals.[9] *Inside Reading* provides multiple exposures to words at varying intervals and recycles vocabulary throughout the book to assist this process.

Learner involvement: Word-learning activities are not guaranteed to be effective simply by virtue of being interactive or communicative. Activities or tasks are most effective when learners are most *involved* in them. Optimal involvement is characterized by a learner's own perceived need for the unknown word, the desire to search for the information needed for the task, and the effort expended to compare the word to other words. It has been found that the greater the level of learner involvement, the better the retention.[10]

The activities in *Inside Reading* provide opportunities to be involved in the use of target words at two levels:

- "Word level," where words are practiced in isolation for the purpose of focusing on such aspects as meaning, derivation, grammatical features, and associations.
- "Sentence level," where learners respond to the readings by writing and paraphrasing sentences.

Because the activities are grounded in the two high-interest readings of each unit, they provide the teacher with frequent opportunities to optimize learner involvement.

Instruction and practice with varying types of word knowledge: To know a word means to know a great deal about the word.[11] The activities in this book include practice with all aspects of word knowledge: form (both oral and written), meaning, multiple meanings, collocations, grammatical features, derivatives, register, and associations.

Helping students become independent word learners: No single course or book can address all of the words a learner will need. Students should leave a class with new skills and strategies for word learning so that they can notice and effectively practice new words as they encounter them. *Inside Reading* includes several features to help guide students to becoming independent word learners. One is a self-assessment activity, which begins and ends each unit. Students evaluate their level of knowledge of each word, ranging from not knowing a word at all, to word recognition, and then to two levels of word use. This exercise demonstrates the incremental nature of word knowledge, and guides learners toward identifying what they know and what they need to know. Students can make better progress if they accurately identify the aspects of word knowledge they need for themselves. Another feature is the use of references and online resources: To further prepare students to be independent word learners, instruction and practice in dictionary use and online resources are provided throughout the book.

The *Inside Reading* Program

Inside Reading offers students and teachers helpful ancillaries:

Student CD-ROM: The CD-ROM in the back of every student book contains additional practice activities for students to work with on their own. The activities are self-correcting and allow students to redo an activity as many times as they wish.

Instructor's pack: The Instructor's Pack contains the answer key for the book along with a test generator CD-ROM. The test generator contains one test per student book unit. Each test consists of a reading passage related to the topic of the unit, which features the target vocabulary. This is followed by reading comprehension and vocabulary questions. Teachers can use each unit's test in full or customize it in a variety of ways.

Inside Reading optimizes the reciprocal relationship between reading and vocabulary by drawing upon considerable research and many years of teaching experience. It provides the resources to help students read well and to use that knowledge to develop both a rich academic vocabulary and overall academic language proficiency.

---

[9] Research findings are inconclusive about the number of repetitions that are needed for retention. Estimates range from 6 to 20. See Nation, 2001, for a discussion of repetition and learning.

[10] Laufer & Hulstijn, 2001

[11] Nation, 1990; 2001

References

Carrel, P.L., Devine, J., & Eskey, D.E. (1988). *Interactive approaches to second language reading*. Cambridge: Cambridge University Press. (Or use "Holding in the bottom" by Eskey)

Coxhead, A. (2000). A new academic word list. *TESOL Quarterly, 34*, 213–238.

Eskey, D.E. (1988). Holding in the bottom. In P.L. Carrel, J. Devine, & D.E. Eskey, *Interactive approaches to second language reading*, pp. 93–100. Cambridge: Cambridge University Press.

Koda, K. (2005). *Insights into second language reading*. Cambridge: Cambridge University Press.

Laufer, B. (2005). Instructed second language vocabulary learning: The fault in the 'default hypothesis'. In A. Housen & M. Pierrard (Eds.), *Investigations in Instructed Second Language Acquisition*, pp. 286–303. New York: Mouton de Gruyter.

Laufer, B. (1992). Reading in a foreign language: How does L2 lexical knowledge interact with the reader's general academic ability? *Journal of Research in Reading, 15*(2), 95–103.

Nation, I.S.P. (1990). *Teaching and learning vocabulary*. New York: Newbury House.

Nation, I.S.P. (2001). *Learning vocabulary in another language*. Cambridge: Cambridge University Press.

Schmidt, R. (1990). The role of consciousness in second language learning. *Applied Linguistics, 11*, 129–158.

Schmitt, N. (2000). *Vocabulary in language teaching*. Cambridge: Cambridge University Press.

Schmitt, N. & Zimmerman, C.B. (2002). Derivative word forms: What do learners know? *TESOL Quarterly, 36*(2), 145–171.

Stahl, S.A. & Fairbanks, M.M. (1986). The effects of vocabulary instruction: A model-based meta-analysis. *Review of Educational Research, 56*(1), 72–110.

Welcome to *Inside Reading*

Inside Reading is a four-level series that develops students' abilities to interact with and access academic reading and vocabulary, preparing them for success in the academic classroom.

There are ten units in *Inside Reading*. Each unit features two readings on a high-interest topic from an academic content area, one or more reading skills and strategies, and work with a set of target word families from the **Academic Word List**.

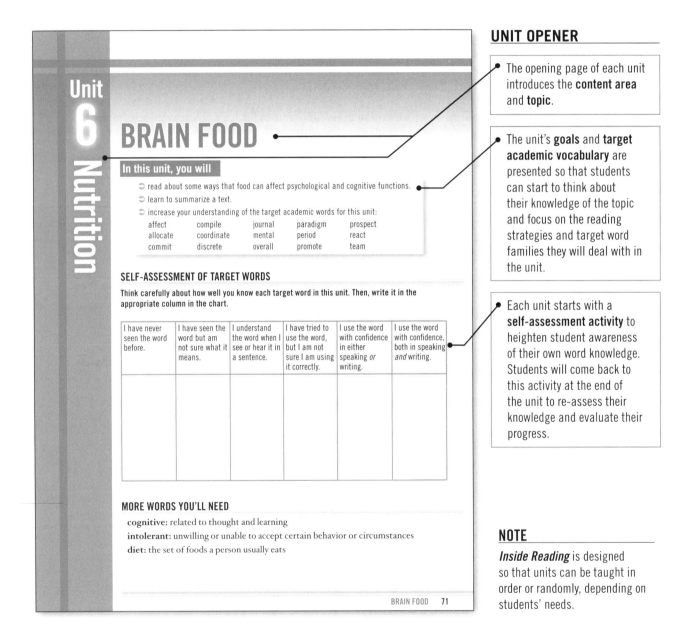

UNIT OPENER

The opening page of each unit introduces the **content area** and **topic**.

The unit's **goals** and **target academic vocabulary** are presented so that students can start to think about their knowledge of the topic and focus on the reading strategies and target word families they will deal with in the unit.

Each unit starts with a **self-assessment activity** to heighten student awareness of their own word knowledge. Students will come back to this activity at the end of the unit to re-assess their knowledge and evaluate their progress.

NOTE

Inside Reading is designed so that units can be taught in order or randomly, depending on students' needs.

Text inside the image:

Unit 6 — Nutrition — BRAIN FOOD

In this unit, you will
- read about some ways that food can affect psychological and cognitive functions.
- learn to summarize a text.
- increase your understanding of the target academic words for this unit:

affect	compile	journal	paradigm	prospect
allocate	coordinate	mental	period	react
commit	discrete	overall	promote	team

SELF-ASSESSMENT OF TARGET WORDS

Think carefully about how well you know each target word in this unit. Then, write it in the appropriate column in the chart.

I have never seen the word before.	I have seen the word but am not sure what it means.	I understand the word when I see or hear it in a sentence.	I have tried to use the word, but I am not sure I am using it correctly.	I use the word with confidence in either speaking *or* writing.	I use the word with confidence, both in speaking *and* writing.

MORE WORDS YOU'LL NEED

cognitive: related to thought and learning
intolerant: unwilling or unable to accept certain behavior or circumstances
diet: the set of foods a person usually eats

BRAIN FOOD   71

READING 1

BEFORE YOU READ

Read these questions. Discuss your answers in a small group.

1. Name three or four foods you often eat even though you know they're not good for you. Why are they unhealthful? Why do you eat them anyway?
2. Name three or four foods you eat that are healthful. Why are they healthful? Do you like the way they taste?
3. Have you ever felt a significant improvement in your mood or in your concentration after a meal or snack? What do you think caused this effect?

READ

This excerpt from a nutrition manual explains the psychological benefits of eating certain fats.

Fat for Brains

As the old saying goes, you are what you eat. The foods you eat obviously **affect** your body's performance. They may also influence how your brain handles its tasks. If it handles them well, you think more clearly and you are more emotionally stable. The right foods can help you concentrate, keep you motivated, sharpen your memory, speed your **reaction** time, defuse stress, and perhaps even prevent brain aging.

Good and bad fat

Most people associate the term *fat* with poor health. We are encouraged to eat fat-free foods and to drain fat away from fried foods. To understand its psychological benefits, however, we have to change the **paradigm** for how we think about fat.

Foods that are high in saturated fats include meat, butter, and other animal products. In general, saturated fats are solid at room temperature. Foods high in unsaturated fats include vegetable oils, nuts, and avocados. Unsaturated fats, if separated out, are usually liquid at room temperature.

Foods high in saturated fats

Before each of the two readings in a unit, students discuss questions to **activate knowledge of the specific topic** dealt with in the reading.

Readings represent **a variety of genres**: newspapers, magazines, websites, press releases, encyclopedias, and books.

Target vocabulary is bold at its first occurrence to aid recognition. **Vocabulary is recycled** and practiced throughout the unit. Target words are also recycled in subsequent units.

READING COMPREHENSION

Reading comprehension questions follow each text to check students' understanding and recycle target vocabulary.

READING COMPREHENSION

Mark each sentence as *T* (true) or *F* (false) according to the information in Reading 1. Use the dictionary to help you understand new words.

.... 1. Foods affect a person's moods and motivation.

.... 2. Ideally, more people should commit to no-fat diets.

.... 3. At room temperature, you could pour unsaturated fat out of a bottle.

.... 4. It is not healthful to eat a very large amount of unsaturated fat.

.... 5. Omega-3 fatty acids promote intellectual development.

.... 6. Breast milk is a better source of DHA than infant formulas.

.... 7. Research journals reported that people with a lot of omega-3 fats in their systems were very depressed.

READING STRATEGIES

Strategy presentation and practice accompanies each reading.

READING STRATEGY: Making Inferences

When you make an inference, you use clues in a reading to understand something the author has not directly stated. The reading implies it, and you infer it. An inference is a conclusion that you draw from the information presented in the reading.

Read the paragraph indicated again. Then, select the one or two statements that can be most strongly inferred from each paragraph. Compare selections with a partner and explain your choices.

1. Paragraph 1:
   a. There are more small tectonic plates than large ones.
   b. The top layer of the mantle is liquid.
   c. The continents were formed from material in the mantle.
2. Paragraph 2:
   a. Catastrophists believed the Earth should not change.
   b. Catastrophists believed religion should not interfere with science.
   c. Catastrophists believed forces we now witness were not enough to shape the Earth.

VOCABULARY ACTIVITIES

The vocabulary work following each reading **starts at word level**. Step I activities are mostly receptive and focus on meanings and word family members.

STEP I VOCABULARY ACTIVITIES: Word Level

A. Read these excerpts from an article on tectonic plates. For each excerpt, cross out the one word or phrase in parentheses with a different meaning from the other three choices. Compare answers with a partner.

1. *Geodesy* is the study of the size and shape of the Earth. Over thousands of years, the tools of the field have (*fluctuated | developed | evolved | progressed*) so that now we can use geodetic measurements to track the movement of tectonic plates.
2. Because plate motions happen all over the globe at the same time, only satellite-based methods can give a truly (*all-inclusive | comprehensive | accurate | thorough*) view of them.
3. In the late 1970s, these space-based techniques completely (*improved | changed | altered | transformed*) the field of geodesy.
4. Of the space-based techniques, the Global Positioning System (GPS) has provided the most (*aid | assistance | truth | help*) to scientists studying the movements of the Earth's crust.
5. By repeatedly measuring distances between specific points, geologists can determine if there has been significant (*displacement | restraint | movement | repositioning*) among the plates.

Vocabulary work then **progresses to the sentence level**. Step II activities are mostly productive and feature work with collocations and specific word usage. These activities can also include work with register, associations, connotations, and learner dictionaries.

STEP II VOCABULARY ACTIVITIES: Sentence Level

Word Form Chart			
Noun	Verb	Adjective	Adverb
transformation	transform	transformative	

D. Answer these questions in your notebook. Use each form of *transform* at least once in your answers. Refer to Reading 1 for information. Compare sentences with a partner.

1. What is the most significant way Earth's landmasses have changed since the days of Pangaea?
2. As scientific thinking became more advanced in Europe, how did explanations of Earth's geology change?
3. How did continental drift affect Antarctica?
4. What role did the theory of plate tectonics play in the debate about continental movement?
5. What big change is likely in the arrangement of Earth's continents?

NOTE

Each unit ends with topics and projects that teachers can use to take the lesson further. This section includes class discussion topics, online research projects, and essay ideas.

Answer Key

Going Underground

Reading 1

Reading Comprehension

1.	T	6.	T
2.	F	7.	F
3.	F	8.	T
4.	T	9.	T
5.	T	10.	F

Step I Vocabulary Activities: Word Level

A.

1. structured   4. creations
2. houses   5. well-known
3. careful

B.

1, 2, 5, and 6. Possible new sentences:

1. The heat and dryness notwithstanding, people like living in Coober Pedy.
2. Notwithstanding the difficulty of building a dug-out, more and more miners want underground homes.
5. Notwithstanding the signs that tell them to be careful, tourists sometimes have accidents in Coober Pedy.
6. Their diverse backgrounds notwithstanding, the people of Coober Pedy work together very well.

Step II Vocabulary Activities: Sentence Level

C.

Answers will vary. Possible answers:

2. Rough behavior is predictable of miners.
3. The weather service would predict hot, dry weather.
4. My prediction is that they will use a drill, a bulldozer, and dynamite.
5. The predicted expansion of the road system would probably not occur.

D.

Answers will vary. Possible answers:

2. The roof of a dugout could collapse if it does not have enough structural support.
3. A harmful gas called radon naturally emerges from the soil into underground spaces.
4. People who live underground should assume that they will have water problems.
5. A builder has to be creative to design an air-circulation system for an underground home.
6. A moist and poorly ventilated underground home is similar to a pile of wet clothes in that both can become moldy.

Reading 2

Reading Comprehension

1.	F	6.	T
2.	T	7.	F
3.	F	8.	F
4.	F	9.	T
5.	F	10.	T

Step I Vocabulary Activities: Word Level

A.

a. unique   d. similar to
b. emerge   e. environment
c. liberal, assume   f. Notwithstanding

B.

Possible order:

1. a   4. d
2. e   5. c
3. f   6. b

C.

1. situate
2.
b. to set up a home or business in a new place
a. to search for and find something
c. to put something into a place
3. *Answers will vary. Possible answer:*
   to find something that was misplaced
4. Correct: a place where a movie is filmed, finding where something is, a site

The Business of Branding

Reading 1

Reading Comprehension

1. T	5. T	9. F
2. T	6. F	10. T
3. T	7. T	
4. F	8. F	

Reading Strategy: Finding the Main Idea

A.

Chunk 2. Branding as a tool for recognition (paragraphs 2 and 3)

Chunk 3. Brands as part of culture (paragraphs 4, 5, and 6)

Chunk 4. Brands and one's self-image (paragraphs 7 and 8)

B.

Paragraph	Signal	Example	An Example of...
Paragraph 2	for example	the Double Jay brand	the branding of animals
Paragraph 4	one prominent case	McDonald's restaurants	companies that have image problems overseas
Paragraph 6	for instance	allowing its name to appear on products or selling advertising space alongside its racetracks	financing NASCAR operations
Paragraph 8	one way	tattooing a logo on one's body	making the Harley-Davidson brand personal

Step I Vocabulary Activities: Word Level

A.

1. revenues
2. converted

4. Departments
5. reward

3. harmed

Step II Vocabulary Activities: Sentence Level

D.

Answers will vary. Possible answers:

1. You have to decide how your brand should reach the consumer.
2. If you advertise, decide how branding fits in with your corporate strategy.
3. What should your product symbolize?
4. AFLAC ran a successful series of ads using a duck as its theme.
5. Teenagers consume styles in very short times, so making a brand work for them is very hard.
6. The government wrongly presumed that teens would pay attention to some anti-drug ads.

E.

1. The symbols register with the brain as cohesive bundles of images.
2. Customers might equate the weakness of the brand with poor quality in the product.
3. License fees finance many of NASCAR's operations.
4. A stronger brand might convert negative perceptions of the product into positive impressions, even if the product itself doesn't change.

Reading 2

Reading Comprehension

1. F	6. F
2. T	7. T
3. F	8. F
4. F	9. T
5. T	10. F

Reading Strategy

Who is A-Ron?	What is aNYthing?	How Branding Works	Products as a Form of Rebellion
A-Ron as a culture expert	labels on T-shirts	companies with stuff to sell	furniture shops
a blog	music, books, and a documentary film	nonconformity or achievement	materialism
south of Delancey Street		the cost of a TV ad	

Step I Vocabulary Activities: Word Level

A.
1. register with
2. convert
3. contradicting
4. consume
5. symbols
6. presumes
7. media
8. themes, equate

B.

1.
a. mechanical energy, heat energy
b. old coal-burning power plants, modern plants
c. Peter Mortenson, a believer of Pangeism
d. ice skate, roller skate.

Step II Vocabulary Activities: Sentence Level

C.

Answers will vary. Possible answers:
1. There is a contradiction between their anti-establishment feelings and their business-oriented actions.
2. They might contradict his portrayal of himself
3. I think it's contradictory to want to sell things but then drive customers away by being rude to them.
4. It's contradictory for them to criticize materialism since they are also promoting materialism with their own products.

UNIT 3
Machines That Recognize Faces

Reading 1

Reading Comprehension
1. T
2. T
3. T
4. F
5. T
6. F

Reading Strategy: Scanning
Answers may vary. Possible answers:
2. near downtown Tampa/Ybor, capital letters/50–52
3. 2001/numbers, 2001, Super Bowl/2
4. a football-related exhibition/capital letters, Experience, NFL/18
5. a society where authorities spy on people/quotation marks, capital letters, society/33–34

Step I Vocabulary Activities: Word Level

A.
1. some data
2. involving
3. Undertaking
4. inside
5. Justifiably
6. modifies

Step II Vocabulary Activities: Sentence Level

C.

Answers will vary. Possible answers:
1. It involved scanning faces in a large crowd.
2. It might be there because of that person's involvement in a crime.
3. Places where the security of people or their possessions is involved.
4. Because it involves measuring (metric) part of a living (bio-) person.
5. It was modified to directly involve the Tampa police database with images recorded by surveillance cameras.

D.

Answers will vary. Possible answers:
1. Critics justifiably question the accuracy of FR technology.
2. The consequence of one study on FR technology was that its findings created controversy within the security industry.
3. People setting up FR systems can't anticipate changes in a person's face.
4. The software is continually being modified, but it is still confused by image changes.
5. As a consequence of long experience recognizing faces, humans are not confused by even large changes in appearance.
6. Are we really justified in spending a lot of money on FR systems when humans are available to do the job better?
7. Most technicians say that creating FR systems does not make sense when they anticipate the problems that might be involved in the process.
8. It is important to consider the consequences that a person's emotions or physical state might have on his or her reliability on an FR task.
9. Although automatic FR systems are controversial, they are still more reliable than people, so modifications should continue to be made to them so they can be used.

Reading 2

Reading Comprehension

1. T		5. T	
2. T		6. F	
3. F		7. T	
4. F		8. T	

Reading Strategy

Answers may vary. Possible answers:

Target Information	Answer	Characters or Keywords	Line(s)
1. What is the full name of the FBI?	The Federal Bureau of Investigation	capital letters	11
2. Where is Logan Airport?	Boston	capital letters; airport	36
3. How many airport workers were pictured in the test database?	40	numbers; airport worker	44
4. What is the NIST?	National Institute for Standards and Technology	NIST	72-73 71-72
5. What is a false positive?	identifying someone as being in the database who is really not there	false positive	53
6. If a system is 94% effective indoors, how effective will it be outdoors?	54%	percentage sign; numbers	83 72
7. How much does a system's reliability decrease each year as a database photo gets older?	about 5% each year	numbers; percentage sign; reliability and decrease	87 86

Step I Vocabulary Activities: Word Level

A.
a. anticipate
b. involved in
c. devices
d. adjacent
e. involving
f. analyzes
g. undertook
h. monitor

B.
Answers may vary. Possible order:

1. a		5. e	
2. d		6. h	
3. b		7. c	
4. g		8. f	

C.
1. examine
2.
a. information
b. traffic problem
c. water
d. purchasing system

UNIT 4
How Could They Do That?

Reading 1

Reading Comprehension

1. T		5. T	
2. T		6. T	
3. F		7. T	
4. T		8. F	

Reading Strategy: Outlining

I. Introduction
II. General description of the Oxford-Stratford debate
   A. Oxfordian position
   B. Stratfordian position
III. Details of the Oxfordian position
   A. Shakespeare's weak background
   B. De Vere's strong background
   C. Evidence from the 1556 Bible
IV. Details of the Stratfordian position
   A. Prominence of Shakespeare's family
   B. Shakespeare's likely attendance at a good school
   C. Shakespeare's prosperity and importance in London
   D. Matching Shakespeare's plays with his life
   E. An unlikely hoax necessary for Oxfordian position
V. The problem of de Vere's 1604 death
   A. Dates of plays after 1604
   B. Oxfordian explanations
VI. Likely future of the debate

Step I Vocabulary Activities: Word Level

A.

1. sculptor's
2. occurred
3. relevant
4. protocols

B.

Correct: 1, 2, 4, 5. Possible new sentences:

3. Shakespeare's move to London preceded his rise to fame.
6. The production of *The Tempest* followed deVere's death.

C.

1. c
2. e
3. a
4. b
5. f
6. d

D.

Answers will vary. Possible answers:

1. Shakespeare's colleagues Hemminge and Condell were named as beneficiaries in the author's will.
2. They eventually compiled a voluminous, 36-play collection called the *First Folio*.
3. Their task was especially difficult because, in the cases of many plays, what Shakespeare meant to say was debatable.

4. In making their decisions, Hemminge and Condell were able to draw on a sustained working relationship with Shakespeare.
5. Nevertheless, the accumulation of errors in the plays made it hard to tell what the original might have said.
6. The end result of their efforts was a 900-page volume entitled *Mr. William Shakespeares Comedies, Histories & Tragedies. Published according to the True Originall Copies*, published in 1623.

F.

Answers will vary. Possible answers:

1. The many complex topics in the plays are indicative of a learned author.
2. It indicates that William Shakespeare probably went to a good school.
3. A strong correlation between them and passages in the plays gives an indication that de Vere might have written the plays.
4. The strength of the evidence is an indicator of the length of the debate. The weaker the evidence, the longer the debate.

Reading 2

Reading Strategy

Answers will vary. One possible outline:

I. Introduction
II. Conrad's childhood
   A. Birth in Poland
   B. Exile to Russia
   C. Death of parents
III. Conrad's early language experience
IV. Conrad's teen years
   A. Dissatisfaction with school
   B. Years as a merchant sailor in France
   C. Suicide attempt
V. Sailing under the British flag
   A. Lack of need for English when a seaman
   B. Need for English to pass tests for promotion
   C. Length of service
VI. Conrad's spoken English
VII. Conrad's written English
VIII. Explanations for Conrad's literary ability in English
   A. A natural feel for the rhythm of English
   B. A psychological attachment to English
IX. Conrad's position in English literature

Reading Comprehension

1. T
2. T
3. F
4. T
5. F
6. F
7. T

Step I Vocabulary Activities: Word Level

A.
1. authors
2. precedes
3. persisted
4. indicates
5. debate
6. reluctant, adequate

B.
1. persist
2. depression
3. adequate
4. indicate
5. volume
6. author

C.
1. Correct: predate.

UNIT 5
Weather Warnings

Reading 1
Reading Comprehension

1. F
2. F
3. T
4. T
5. F
6. T
7. F
8. T
9. F
10. T

Reading Strategy: Reading Graphs

1. January
2. July
3. June
4. January & February
5. January & February, and May & August
6. February & December
7. In general, average precipitation increases as average temperature increases.
8. *Answers will vary.*

Step I Vocabulary Activities: Word Level

A.
1. extremes
2. routes
3. strategy
4. orient
5. reinforce
6. engaging
7. indicate
8. energized

Step II Vocabulary Activities: Sentence Level

D.
Answers will vary. Possible answers:
1. She said she saw the defendant gesturing energetically.
2. Because the sound energy would not have reached her ears.
3. Their denial of his claim energized him to take some action.
4. The energy from the falling hail is directed from above, not from the sides, and would affect the roof, the hood, and the trunk.
5. Any energetic entrepreneur can become one.
6. A meteorologist should understand the energy of different weather phenomena.

E.
Answers will vary. Possible answers:
1. A coherent explanation.
2. Phenomena in space.
3. Lightning storms exhibited them.
4. Through assistance from the National Science Foundation.
5. They are examining them sectionally.
6. They are tropical phenomena.

Reading 2
Reading Comprehension

1. T
2. T
3. F
4. F
5. T
6. T
7. F
8. T

Reading Strategy

A.
1. Between the middle stage and the late stage.
2. The early stage.
3. The wind direction shifts in a counter-clockwise direction from west to northwest.
4. Between the middle and late stages.

Step I Vocabulary Activities: Word Level

A.
1. disoriented
2. energy
3. phenomenon
4. section
5. exhibit
6. reinforces

B.
1. previous
2. exhibit
3. reinforce
4. route
5. core
6. interval

C.
1. Correct: direct
2.
a. informational meeting
b. confused
c. point in the right direction
d. suitable

UNIT 6
Brain Food

Reading 1
Reading Comprehension
1. T
2. F
3. T
4. T
5. T
6. T
7. F
8. T

Reading Strategy: Summarizing
A.

Answers may vary. Possible answers:
A balance of fats, brain cells, IQ and depression, omega-3s, saturated and unsaturated fats

Step I Vocabulary Activities: Word Level
A.
1. caused
2. complete
3. convert
4. finally
5. sponsor
6. sections
7. wrote

Step II Vocabulary Activities: Sentence Level
D.

Answers will vary. Possible answers:
2. e, I can't meet at that time because I have a commitment.
3. d, She is totally committed to her daughter.
4. b, He suffered from depression for many years and finally committed suicide.
5. j, His leaving early shows a lack of commitment to the team.
6. g, The government honored its commitment to provide more money for the school lunch program.
7. a, He went to prison for committing crimes.
8. c, She thinks she can come tomorrow, but she won't commit herself until she talks to her sister.
9. f, They would love to take a vacation, but they have a lot of other commitments.
10. h, He's not really sick. He's just trying to get out of commitment.

E.

Answers will vary. Possible answers:
1. Antioxidants in the diet may help keep older people mentally sharp.
2. Antioxidants react with free radicals and reduce their ability to damage bodily tissue.
3. The overall effect of free radicals is to promote the deterioration in body tissues that we associate with aging.
4. One of the most disturbing things about aging is how it affects the brain.
5. Some older people have improved their prospects of staying sharp by eating foods high in antioxidants.
6. The cognitive abilities of older people who take anti-oxidants in pill form, however, seem to be unaffected by the supplements.

Reading 2
Reading Comprehension
1. F
2. T
3. F
4. T
5. F
6. T
7. F
8. T

Step I Vocabulary Activities: Word Level
A.
1. period
2. compile
3. journal
4. allocate
5. discrete
6. promote

B.
a. affect
b. compiled
c. paradigm
d. reacted
e. prospect
f. coordination
g. promote, overall
h. mental

C.

Answers may vary. Possible order:
1. c
2. h
3. d
4. e
5. b
6. g
7. a
8. f

D.
1. Correct: organize
2.
a. the operations
b. outfits
c. the hand and the eye
d. athletic events

E.

Answers will vary. Possible answers.

1. A person's life can be divided into a few discrete time periods (infancy, childhood, adolescence, adulthood, old age).
2. A college career usually goes through a series of discrete levels (freshman, sophomore, junior, senior).
3. Nurses are responsible for many discrete hospital operations (monitoring vital signs, treating injuries, giving medication).
4. The Minnesota Starvation Experiment was broken into three discrete stages (adequate diet, semi-starvation, recovery).
5. The people in my life promote my health and well-being in discrete ways (exercising with me, engaging in social activities with me, showing concern for me).

UNIT 7
Roving Continents

Reading 1
Reading Comprehension

1. T	6. T
2. F	7. F
3. T	8. T
4. F	9. T
5. T	10. T

Reading Strategy: Making Inferences

Answers may vary. Possible answers:

1. b	3. a & b
2. a & c	4. a & c

Step I Vocabulary Activities: Word Level

1. fluctuated	5. restraint
2. accurate	6. rigidly
3. improved	7. evolve
4. truth	

B.

Answers will vary. Possible answers:

1. several divisions, individual soldiers
2. lawn, trees, track, playground
3. many of the countries in Europe
4. railway lines, highways, airports
5. several highly skilled players
6. several blocks, individual homes

Step II Vocabulary Activities: Sentence Level
D.

Answers will vary. Possible answers:

1. They have transformed from one continent into seven.
2. It led to a transformation from catastrophist beliefs to uniformitarian beliefs.
3. Antarctica was transformed from a mild place where plants could grow into a cold, barren place.
4. It was transformative, turning a theory that seemed physically impossible into one that seemed probable.
5. Earth's continents will probably undergo a transformation into one supercontinent again.

E.

Answers will vary. Possible answers:

1. Some geologists, unwilling to be restrained by the past, are thinking far into the future.
2. They are trying to use plate tectonics to see how the Earth might evolve in the next 250 million years.
3. Dr. Christopher Scotese envisions the evolution of a new supercontinent, which he calls Pangaea Ultima.
4. Many geologists predict that the Mediterranean Sea will be displaced by a new mountain range as Africa collides with Europe.
5. After Australia and Antarctica collide with Afrasia, only a small area will be left to accommodate the Indian Ocean.
6. As South America moves north, it will displace the Caribbean islands.
7. Scotese predicts that the movement of the Americas will eventually reverse, so that they will start heading east toward Afrasia and displace the Atlantic Ocean.
8. Other geologists predict no restraint on westward movement by the Americas, causing the Pacific Ocean to eventually disappear.

9. When making predictions about the next 250 million years, one must be prepared to accommodate many surprises.

Reading 2

Reading Comprehension
1. T
2. F
3. T
4. T
5. F
6. ~~F~~ T
7. T
8. T
9. F
10. F

Reading Strategy
1. unscientific
2. perceptive
3. accurate
4. useful
5. inevitable

Step I Vocabulary Activities: Word Level
A.
a. evolving
b. accommodated
c. an intermediate
d. displacement
e. restrain
f. community
g. aided
h. fluctuated

B.
Answers may vary. Possible order:
1. g
2. e
3. a
4. b
5. h
6. d
7. f
8. c

D.
1. Correct: suit
2.
a. the family
b. Jim's disability
c. the party's demands
d. the press

UNIT 8
Clicks and Cliques

Reading 1

Reading Comprehension
1. F
2. T
3. F
4. T
5. F
6. F
7. T
8. F

Reading Strategy: Highlighting and Annotating
1. University of Evansville
2. Ohio
3. 7.5 million
4. 22,000
5. MySpace
6. acting like someone you're not
7. Tim McGraw & Faith Hill
8. Sarah B. Westfall

Step I Vocabulary Activities: Word Level
A.
1. display
2. cute
3. source
4. dear
5. dialect
6. questionable

B.
Answers may vary. Possible answers:
1. hate
2. old age
3. sadness
4. failure
5. aggression
6. unpredictability

Step II Vocabulary Activities: Sentence Level
D.
Answers will vary. Possible answers:
1. Most college freshmen expect to get along with their roommates. They are surprised when things turn out conversely.
2. Part of the problem is that some freshmen think a roommate is guaranteed to become their friend by the university.
3. Inevitably, two new students with no other friends available will look to each other for support.
4. After a few weeks on campus, however, each roommate's group of friends and acquaintances will diversify.
5. A problem can develop if one of the roommates is socially passive, or unwilling to go out and seek new friends.
6. If a college orientation program is honest about the inevitability of roommate separation, there will be less anxiety.
7. Freshmen who are socially successful can give some social assistance to their roommates who are the converse.
8. One roommate cannot be expected to give a friendship guarantee to the other, since

college students ought to have social skills of their own.

E.

Answers will vary. Possible answers:

1. They are unsure how to react to behavior that deviates from what they are familiar with.
2. Telling little lies on a social networking site is not deviant behavior. Everybody does it.
3. It would be a real deviation from the norm for a college to let freshmen choose their own roommates.
4. The student and his or her parents would certainly warn the college that the roommate might be a deviant.
5. The style of Sarah's website deviated from what Brandi liked.

Reading 2

Reading Comprehension

1.	T	5.	T
2.	F	6.	T
3.	F	7.	F
4.	T	8.	T

Step I Vocabulary Activities: Word Level

A.
- a. inevitable
- b. so-called
- c. domain
- d. gender
- e. instituted
- f. deviate
- g. guaranteed
- h. intervene

B.

Answers may vary. Possible order:

a, c, d, g, e, f, h, b

C.

1.	arbitrary	4.	converse
2.	deviate	5.	inevitable
3.	intervene		

D.

1. Correct: variegated
2.
   a. opinion
   b. cultures of students

c. range of products
d. set of investments

True and False

Reading 1

Reading Comprehension

1.	F	6.	T
2.	T	7.	F
3.	T	8.	T
4.	F	9.	T
5.	F	10.	T

Reading Strategy: Understanding Sequences

Answers will vary. Possible answers:

The Voricks
- a. The alleged "terrorist" lives in the house the Voricks would buy.
- b. The Voricks buy the house and the alleged "terrorist" moves elsewhere.
- c. A news commentator says on TV that a terrorist lives at the Voricks' address.
- d. People harass the Voricks.

The New Yorker
- a. The magazine is known for excellent fact-checking.
- b. The quality of fact-checking at the magazine declines.
- c. Tina Brown becomes managing editor.
- d. The fact-checking department once again becomes famously thorough.

The Newsweek story
- a. A single source tells the magazine about misbehavior by soldiers.
- b. Newsweek publishes a story about it.
- c. Riots over the report kill more than a dozen people.
- d. No one can be found to confirm the story.
- e. Newsweek retracts the story.

Step I Vocabulary Activities: Word Level

A.

1.	clearly	5.	hopes
2.	expert	6.	amended
3.	admit	7.	showed up for
4.	unethically	8.	accept

B.

1. d	5. h
2. e	6. f
3. g	7. c
4. a	8. b

Step II Vocabulary Activities: Sentence Level

D.

Answers will vary. Possible answers:

1. The driver was in a hurry so he ignored the speed limit.
2. The driver said he was ignorant of a change in the speed limit, but still got a ticket.
3. The police officer told him that ignorance of the law was no excuse.
4. While the reporter was in Malawi, she embarrassed herself several times because she was ignorant of local customs.
5. The editor dropped the story because she thought the reporter had deliberately ignored some information.
6. The editor said that ignoring a problem will not make it go away.

E.

Answers will vary. Possible answers:

1. A Washington Post reporter submitted a story about a child drug addict.
2. Janet Cooke, the reporter, was granted a Pulitzer Prize for the story.
3. Washington's mayor assigned dozens of people to look for the child.
4. It soon became apparent that he probably did not exist.
5. Successive investigations found several untruths in the story and in other statements by Cooke.
6. Shortly after the prize was given, the Post had to submit to the obvious and apologize for the fake story.
7. Cooke quit and gave back the prize, but she assigned blame to her editors.
8. Katherine Graham's successor in the Post's top spot, her son Dan, put procedures in place to more closely screen reporters who want to work for the paper.

Reading 2

Reading Comprehension

1. F	6. F
2. T	7. T

3. F	8. F
4. T	9. T
5. T	10. T

Reading Strategy

A.

Answers may vary. Possible answers (in order):

photographer taking pictures
photographer altering pictures
photographer selling them to news service
news service distributing photos
errors discovered in photos
news service stopping distribution of photos

Step I Vocabulary Activities: Word Level

A.

a. emphasize	e. successor
b. amend	f. an apparently,
c. restrict	ignores
d. perceived	g. eliminated
	h. inserted

B.

Answers may vary. Possible order:

c, d, h, f, e, a, b, g

C.

1. purchase	4. perceive
2. eliminate	5. submit
3. grant	6. amend

D.

1.
Meaning 1: offer
Meaning 2: defer
2.
Meaning 1: a and b
Meaning 2: c and d

UNIT 10

Bites and Stings

Reading 1

Reading Comprehension

1. F	6. T
2. F	7. F
3. T	8. T
4. F	9. T
5. F	10. F

Step I Vocabulary Activities: Word Level

A.

1. venoms	5. local

2. no
3. beneficial
4. desirable
6. argue
7. Especially

8. Still, it is unlikely that any human effort would be sufficient to make a big dent in the threat malaria presents.

Step II Vocabulary Activities: Sentence Level

C.
Answers will vary. Possible answers:
1. Scientists estimate there are more than 80 thousand species.
2. An estimated 30 percent to 60 percent will get bitten.
3. He has underestimated the length of treatment.
4. That the state official is overestimating the threat they posed by the ants.
5. No. In my estimation, living in Arizona would be dangerous for that person.

D.
Answers will vary. Possible answers:
1. The bites of non-venomous insects can initiate more serious illnesses than the bites of venomous ones.
2. Venomous insects make up only a minimal proportion of all the insects on Earth.
3. The bite of a non-venomous insect is not sufficiently dangerous to cause a problem.
4. The insect is just a neutral carrier of the micro-organism that is truly harmful.
5. About 40 percent of the people on Earth live in circumstances where they could be bitten by disease-carrying mosquitoes.
6. Venoms can usually be neutralized, but vector-borne diseases can't.
7. Governments and non-profits have launched serious anti-malarial initiatives.

Reading 2

Reading Comprehension
1. F
2. T
3. T
4. F
5. T
6. F
7. F
8. F
9. F
10. F

Step I Vocabulary Activities: Word Level

A.
1. append
2. sufficient
3. estimate
4. external
5. initiate

B.
a. chemicals
b. sufficient
c. neutral
d. circumstantial, percentage
e. minimal
f. in contact with
g. regime
h. initiates

C.
Answers may vary. Possible order:
a, f, g, d, b, h, e, c

D.
1. Correct: conditions
2.
a. us and our plans
b. an offer of something to do
c. his presence at the store
d. his disappearance

Inside Reading 2

The Academic Word List
(words targeted in Level 2 are bold)

Word	Sublist	Location	Word	Sublist	Location	Word	Sublist	Location
abandon	8	L1, U7	attain	9	L1, U5	complex	2	L4, U2
abstract	6	L3, U5	attitude	4	L4, U6	component	3	L4, U3
academy	5	L3, U1	attribute	4	L3, U10	compound	5	L4, U6
access	4	L1, U2	**author**	**6**	**L2, U4**	**comprehensive**	**7**	**L2, U7**
accommodate	**9**	**L2, U7**	authority	1	L1, U6	comprise	7	L4, U9
accompany	8	L1, U2	automate	8	L3, U6	compute	2	L4, U8
accumulate	**8**	**L2, U4**	available	1	L3, U5	conceive	10	L4, U10
accurate	6	L4, U6	aware	5	L1, U5	concentrate	4	L3, U8
achieve	2	L4, U1				concept	1	L3, U1
acknowledge	6	L1, U7	behalf	9	L3, U9	conclude	2	L1, U6
acquire	2	L1, U4	benefit	1	L4, U2	concurrent	9	L4, U5
adapt	7	L4, U7	bias	8	L4, U8	conduct	2	L1, U9
adequate	**4**	**L2, U4**	bond	6	L4, U3	confer	4	L4, U4
adjacent	**10**	**L2, U3**	brief	6	L3, U6	confine	9	L1, U10
adjust	5	L4, U3	bulk	9	L4, U9	confirm	7	L4, U10
administrate	2	L1, U3				conflict	5	L1, U2
adult	7	L3, U6	capable	6	L1, U8	conform	8	L4, U7
advocate	7	L1, U10	capacity	5	L4, U9	consent	3	L4, U7
affect	**2**	**L2, U6**	category	2	L4, U5	**consequent**	**2**	**L2, U3**
aggregate	6	L1, U9	cease	9	L4, U10	considerable	3	L3, U8
aid	**7**	**L2, U7**	challenge	5	L3, U8	consist	1	L4, U2, U9
albeit	10	L1, U7	channel	7	L1, U3	constant	3	L4, U8
allocate	**6**	**L2, U6**	chapter	2	L3, U7	constitute	1	L1, U4
alter	5	L1, U1	chart	8	L3, U10	constrain	3	L1, U8
alternative	3	L1, U10	**chemical**	**7**	**L2, U10**	construct	2	L3, U1
ambiguous	8	L1, U4	**circumstance**	**3**	**L2, U10**	consult	5	L1, U6
amend	**5**	**L2, U9**	cite	6	L4, U10	**consume**	**2**	**L2, U2**
analogy	9	L1, U4	civil	4	L1, U4	**contact**	**5**	**L2, U10**
analyze	**1**	**L2, U3**	clarify	8	L4, U8	contemporary	8	L1, U7
annual	4	L1, U9	classic	7	L3, U9	context	1	L1, U4
anticipate	**9**	**L2, U3**	**clause**	**5**	**L2, U8**	contract	1	L3, U9
apparent	**4**	**L2, U9**	code	4	L4, U9	**contradict**	**8**	**L2, U2**
append	**8**	**L2, U10**	**coherent**	**9**	**L2, U5**	contrary	7	L1, U6
appreciate	8	L3, U5	coincide	9	L1, U5	contrast	4	L1, U7
approach	1	L3, U1	collapse	10	L4, U10	contribute	3	L1, U9
appropriate	2	L1, U8	colleague	10	L1, U5	**controversy**	**9**	**L2, U3**
approximate	4	L3, U4	commence	9	L3, U9	convene	3	L1, U4
arbitrary	**8**	**L2, U8**	comment	3	L3, U3	**converse**	**9**	**L2, U8**
area	1	L4, U1	commission	2	L3, U9	**convert**	**7**	**L2, U2**
aspect	2	L3, U4	**commit**	**4**	**L2, U6**	convince	10	L1, U3
assemble	10	L3, U10	commodity	8	L4, U6	cooperate	6	L1, U2
assess	1	L1, U8	communicate	4	L3, U2	**coordinate**	**3**	**L2, U6**
assign	**6**	**L2, U9**	**community**	**2**	**L2, U7**	**core**	**3**	**L2, U5**
assist	**2**	**L2, U5**	compatible	9	L1, U9	**corporate**	**3**	**L2, U2**
assume	**1**	**L2, U1**	compensate	3	L3, U4	correspond	3	L3, U9
assure	9	L3, U4	**compile**	**10**	**L2, U6**	couple	7	L3, U1
attach	6	L3, U7	complement	8	L1, U7	**create**	**1**	**L2, U1**

Word	Sublist	Location	Word	Sublist	Location	Word	Sublist	Location
crucial	8	L3, U10	energy	5	**L2, U5**	fundamental	5	L4, U4
culture	2	L4, U10	enforce	5	L4, U7	furthermore	6	L4, U9
currency	8	L3, U9	enhance	6	L3, U1			
cycle	4	L4, U5	enormous	10	L3, U8	**gender**	6	**L2, U8**
			ensure	3	**L2, U5**	generate	5	L1, U5
data	1	**L2, U3**	entity	5	L4, U5	generation	5	L1, U7
debate	4	**L2, U4**	**environment**	1	**L2, U1**	globe	7	L3, U2
decade	7	L1, U7	**equate**	2	**L2, U2**	goal	4	L3, U3
decline	5	L1, U2	**equip**	7	**L2, U3**	grade	7	L1, U7
deduce	3	L4, U7	equivalent	5	L3, U10	**grant**	4	**L2, U9**
define	1	L3, U2	erode	9	L1, U9	**guarantee**	7	**L2, U8**
definite	7	L3, U4	error	4	L1, U10	guideline	8	L3, U3
demonstrate	3	L1, U5	establish	1	L1, U6			
denote	8	L4, U6	estate	6	L4, U6	hence	4	L3, U5
deny	7	L4, U10	**estimate**	1	**L2, U10**	hierarchy	7	L3, U4
depress	10	**L2, U4**	**ethic**	9	**L2, U9**	highlight	8	L4, U3
derive	1	L4, U10	**ethnic**	4	**L2, U1**	hypothesis	4	L4, U7
design	2	L1, U1	evaluate	2	L1, U10			
despite	4	L3, U2	eventual	8	L4, U3	identical	7	L4, U5
detect	8	L1, U6	evident	1	L4, U2	identify	1	L4, U2
deviate	8	**L2, U8**	**evolve**	5	**L2, U7**	ideology	7	L4, U6
device	9	**L2, U3**	exceed	6	L4, U1	**ignorance**	6	**L2, U9**
devote	9	L3, U9	exclude	3	L4, U7	illustrate	3	L4, U9
differentiate	7	L1, U4	**exhibit**	8	**L2, U5**	image	5	L3, U5
dimension	4	L4, U5	expand	5	L1, U7	**immigrate**	3	**L2, U1**
diminish	9	L4, U4	expert	6	L3, U8	impact	2	L1, U9
discrete	5	**L2, U6**	explicit	6	L1, U3	implement	4	L1, U2
discriminate	6	L1, U10	exploit	8	L1, U5	implicate	4	L4, U7
displace	8	**L2, U7**	export	1	L1, U3	implicit	8	L1, U3
display	6	L3, U5	expose	5	L3, U5	imply	3	L4, U7
dispose	7	L4, U6	**external**	5	**L2, U10**	impose	4	L1, U10
distinct	2	L3, U7	extract	7	L3, U2	incentive	6	L1, U10
distort	9	L3, U6				incidence	6	L3, U10
distribute	1	L4, U8	facilitate	5	L4, U1	incline	10	L1, U7
diverse	6	**L2, U8**	factor	1	L3, U8	income	1	L1, U3
document	3	L4, U9	feature	2	L4, U1	incorporate	6	L4, U4
domain	6	**L2, U8**	**federal**	6	**L2, U3**	index	6	L1, U4
domestic	4	L1, U3	fee	6	L1, U1	**indicate**	1	**L2, U4**
dominate	3	L1, U5	file	7	L4, U6	individual	1	L1, U1
draft	5	L3, U6	final	2	L4, U3	induce	8	L3, U7
drama	8	L3, U5	**finance**	1	**L2, U2**	**inevitable**	8	**L2, U8**
duration	9	L4, U1	finite	7	L1, U9	infer	7	L1, U8
dynamic	7	L1, U5	flexible	6	L3, U9	infrastructure	8	L4, U6
			fluctuate	8	**L2, U7**	inherent	9	L1, U1
economy	1	L1, U7	focus	2	L3, U8	inhibit	6	L1, U5
edit	6	L4, U8	format	9	L4, U8	initial	3	L3, U7
element	2	L4, U1	formula	1	L4, U8	**initiate**	6	**L2, U10**
eliminate	7	**L2, U9**	forthcoming	10	L4, U3	injure	2	L1, U1
emerge	4	**L2, U1**	found	9	L4, U8	innovate	7	L1, U3
emphasis	3	**L2, U9**	foundation	7	L4, U4	input	6	L3, U6
empirical	7	L3, U4	framework	3	L1, U1	**insert**	7	**L2, U9**
enable	5	L3, U10	function	1	L3, U1	insight	9	L3, U7
encounter	10	L3, U5	fund	3	L3, U3	inspect	8	L3, U3

Word	Sublist	Location	Word	Sublist	Location	Word	Sublist	Location
instance	3	L1, U6	mental	5	L2, U6	period	1	L2, U6
institute	2	L2, U8	method	1	L4, U9	persist	10	L2, U4
instruct	6	L4, U2	migrate	6	L3, U2	perspective	5	L3, U2
integral	9	L1, U4	military	9	L1, U4	phase	4	L1, U8
integrate	4	L2, U7	minimal	9	L2, U10	phenomenon	7	L2, U5
integrity	10	L3, U7	minimize	8	L1, U1	philosophy	3	L4, U5
intelligence	6	L3, U8	minimum	6	L4, U5	physical	3	L4, U4
intense	8	L1, U2	ministry	6	L1, U2	plus	8	L4, U5
interact	3	L1, U8	minor	3	L3, U7	policy	1	L3, U3
intermediate	9	L2, U7	mode	7	L4, U7	portion	9	L3, U9
internal	4	L3, U7	modify	5	L2, U3	pose	10	L3, U1
interpret	1	L3, U3	monitor	5	L2, U3	positive	2	L1, U5
interval	6	L2, U5	motive	6	L1, U6	potential	2	L4, U8
intervene	7	L2, U8	mutual	9	L3, U3	practitioner	8	L1, U2
intrinsic	10	L4, U4				precede	6	L2, U4
invest	2	L2, U4	negate	3	L4, U2	precise	5	L3, U10
investigate	4	L4, U8	network	5	L3, U2	predict	4	L2, U1
invoke	10	L1, U3	neutral	6	L2, U10	predominant	8	L1, U8
involve	1	L2, U3	nevertheless	6	L4, U10	preliminary	9	L4, U1
isolate	7	L3, U4	nonetheless	10	L4, U7	presume	6	L2, U2
issue	1	L4, U2	norm	9	L4, U6	previous	2	L2, U5
item	2	L3, U10	normal	2	L3, U8;	primary	2	L1, U1
					L4, U2	prime	5	L4, U4
job	4	L1, U1	notion	5	L4, U9	principal	4	L4, U5
journal	2	L2, U6	notwithstanding	10	L2, U1	principle	1	L3, U9
justify	3	L2, U3	nuclear	8	L2, U7	prior	4	L3, U6
						priority	7	L1, U2
label	4	L2, U2	objective	5	L1, U10	proceed	1	L4, U9
labor	1	L1, U2	obtain	2	L3, U6	process	1	L1, U9
layer	3	L3, U4	obvious	4	L3, U7	professional	4	L1, U5
lecture	6	L4, U2	occupy	4	L1, U9	prohibit	7	L3, U10
legal	1	L2, U3	occur	1	L1, U2	project	4	L4, U4,U9
legislate	1	L3, U3	odd	10	L1, U8	promote	4	L2, U6
levy	10	L2, U9	offset	8	L4, U8	proportion	3	L1, U10
liberal	5	L2, U1	ongoing	10	L3, U3	prospect	8	L2, U6
license	5	L3, U9	option	4	L4, U7	protocol	9	L2, U4
likewise	10	L4, U5	orient	5	L2, U5	psychology	5	L4, U2
link	3	L1, U8	outcome	3	L3, U4	publication	7	L3, U1
locate	3	L2, U1	output	4	L1, U7	publish	3	L1, U3
logic	5	L1, U6	overall	4	L2, U6	purchase	2	L2, U9
			overlap	9	L1, U7	pursue	5	L3, U8
maintain	2	L4, U1	overseas	6	L1, U1			
major	1	L3, U2				qualitative	9	L3, U9
manipulate	8	L4, U4	panel	10	L1, U6	quote	7	L4, U10
manual	9	L3, U10	paradigm	7	L2, U6			
margin	5	L4, U3	paragraph	8	L3, U6	radical	8	L3, U4
mature	9	L1, U8	parallel	4	L3, U9	random	8	L2, U7
maximize	3	L2, U8	parameter	4	L4, U5	range	2	L3, U1
mechanism	4	L3, U9	participate	2	L1, U8	ratio	5	L1, U8
media	7	L1, U5	partner	3	L3, U1	rational	6	L3, U3
mediate	9	L4, U2	passive	9	L2, U8	react	3	L2, U6
medical	5	L1, U2	perceive	2	L2, U9	recover	6	L3, U4
medium	9	L2, U2	percent	1	L2, U10	refine	9	L4, U4

Word	Sublist	Location
regime	4	**L2, U10**
region	2	L3, U1
register	3	**L2, U2**
regulate	2	L3, U6
reinforce	8	**L2, U5**
reject	5	L1, U7
relax	9	L1, U8
release	7	L4, U1
relevant	2	L4, U8
reluctance	10	**L2, U4**
rely	3	L3, U2
remove	3	L3, U2
require	1	L4, U2
research	1	L4, U2
reside	2	L1, U2
resolve	4	L3, U4
resource	2	L3, U8
respond	1	L4, U7
restore	8	L3, U5
restrain	9	**L2, U7**
restrict	2	**L2, U9**
retain	4	L4, U3
reveal	6	L3, U8
revenue	5	**L2, U2**
reverse	7	**L2, U7**
revise	8	L3, U6
revolution	9	L1, U1
rigid	9	**L2, U7**
role	1	L1, U5
route	9	**L2, U5**
scenario	9	L3, U7
schedule	8	L4, U9
scheme	3	L4, U3
scope	6	L4, U8
section	1	**L2, U5**
sector	1	L1, U3
secure	2	L4, U6
seek	2	L4, U3
select	2	L3, U1
sequence	3	L3, U5
series	4	L3, U5
sex	3	L1, U3
shift	3	L4, U9
significant	1	L3, U10
similar	1	**L2, U1**
simulate	7	L3, U1
site	2	L1, U6
so-called	10	**L2, U8**
sole	7	L4, U1
somewhat	7	L1, U4
source	1	L3, U2

Word	Sublist	Location
specific	1	L1, U6
specify	3	L4, U6
sphere	9	L3, U7
stable	5	L4, U5
statistic	4	L4, U7
status	4	L3, U2
straightforward	10	L3, U4
strategy	2	**L2, U5**
stress	4	L4, U4
structure	1	**L2, U1**
style	5	L1, U4
submit	7	**L2, U9**
subordinate	9	L4, U3
subsequent	4	L1, U1
subsidy	6	**L2, U2**
substitute	5	L1, U1
successor	7	**L2, U9**
sufficient	3	**L2, U10**
sum	4	L1, U10
summary	4	**L2, U10**
supplement	9	L4, U10
survey	2	L1, U3
survive	7	L3, U2
suspend	9	L1, U10
sustain	5	**L2, U4**
symbol	5	**L2, U2**
tape	6	L1, U6
target	5	L3, U10
task	3	L1, U8
team	9	**L2, U6**
technical	3	L1, U6
technique	3	**L2, U1**
technology	3	L3, U8
temporary	9	L1, U9
tense	8	L1, U10
terminate	8	L1, U9
text	2	**L2, U4**
theme	8	**L2, U2**
theory	1	L4, U4
thereby	8	L4, U3
thesis	7	L4, U7
topic	7	L3, U3
trace	6	L1, U9
tradition	2	L3, U6
transfer	2	L4, U1
transform	6	**L2, U7**
transit	5	L3, U5
transmit	7	L4, U4
transport	6	L4, U10
trend	5	L4, U6
trigger	9	L3, U7

Word	Sublist	Location
ultimate	7	L1, U9
undergo	10	L4, U1
underlie	6	L4, U6
undertake	4	**L2, U3**
uniform	8	L3, U1
unify	9	L4, U5
unique	7	**L2, U1**
utilize	6	L3, U8
valid	3	L4, U10
vary	1	L3, U10
vehicle	8	L4, U3
version	5	L3, U5
via	8	L1, U4
violate	9	L3, U6
virtual	8	**L2, U10**
visible	7	L3, U5
vision	9	L4, U3
visual	8	L3, U7
volume	3	**L2, U4**
voluntary	7	L1, U10
welfare	5	L4, U1
whereas	5	L4, U2
whereby	10	L1, U4
widespread	8	L4, U10

Notes

Notes

Notes

Notes

Notes

Installation Instructions

Close all programs before installing Diploma.

Installing and opening Diploma using Windows

1. Insert the Diploma CD-ROM in your computer CD drive.

2. If your computer is configured to install CD-ROMs automatically,
   - the Diploma installation screen will appear
   - click the "Install Diploma" option and follow the instructions as they appear on screen
   - click "Exit" when you are done.

   If your computer is not configured to install CD-ROMs automatically,
   - run the Setup Program by clicking on Windows "Start" button
   - select the "Run" option
   - in the box marked "Open," type "D:\Setup\DiplomaSetup.exe" (where "D" is the letter for the CD drive)
   - click OK
   - follow the instructions in the Diploma installation wizard.

   The software will be installed on your hard drive. You will need to restart your computer at the end of the install.

3. To open Diploma,
   - click the "Start" button
   - select the "Programs" option
   - choose "Diploma 6"
   - select the question bank that you want to use.

Installing and opening Diploma using Macintosh

1. Insert the Diploma CD-ROM in your computer CD drive.

2. A folder of the CD-ROM's contents should appear. If the folder doesn't appear, double-click the CD icon.

3. Double-click the "Diploma 6 for Mac OS X" icon. Follow the instructions as they appear on screen. The software will be installed on your hard drive.

4. To open Diploma,
   - double-click on your hard drive icon
   - open the "Applications" folder
   - locate the "Diploma 6" program
   - double-click it to launch Diploma
   - a window showing available question banks will appear.